IMAGES
of Wales

MORRISTON

On their way to the Salvation Army *c.* 1959. Left to right: Margaret Harris, Gloria Mead, Moira Williams and Joan Gower.

IMAGES
of Wales

MORRISTON

André Scoville

TEMPUS

An 1896 view of Church Street, later renamed Lower Morfydd Street.

First published 2002

Tempus Publishing Limited
The Mill, Brimscombe Port,
Stroud, Gloucestershire, GL5 2QG

British Library Cataloguing in Publication Data.
A catalogue record for this book is available from the British Library.

ISBN 0 7524 2666 4

Typesetting and origination by Tempus Publishing Limited
Printed in Great Britain by Midway Colour Print, Wiltshire

Contents

Morriston owes its name and creation to Sir John Morris, Baronet of Clasemont, (1745-1819) pictured left. His home at Clasemont was visited by Lord Nelson and Lord and Lady Hamilton in 1802. He was also one of the founder committee members of the original Mumbles Passenger Railway in 1804.

The original streets of Morriston that are still clearly visible today are constructed on a grid layout to the designs of Revd William Edwards (1719-1789). He was responsible for building the first Wychtree Bridge, built in 1796 and demolished in 1959. This was a truly remarkable man.

Introduction

Over the last fifteen years I have written extensively about the history of Morriston. I'm sure everyone knows that the town was named after Sir John Morris, Baronet of Clasemont, who resided at a mansion house at Clasemont in the mid-1700s in the region of the DVLA. His father, Robert Morris, owned many copper works in the Swansea area and thought of the idea to build a block of flats at Trewyddfa for his workers, the remains of which can still be seen today from Landore. His second son John bought Brookes' land in 1768 and, with the assistance of Revd William Edwards, designed a new grid layout of streets thus creating a new town called Morris' Town.

In his 1819 book, Revd T. Rees stated;

> This is a large straggling village, built for the accommodation of the persons employed in the numerous collieries, copper works, etc, in the neighbourhood. The houses for the poor class of population are of a very excellent and commodious construction, and are ranged in straight lines, with a view to regularity of plan in the streets, in case their number should in time be sufficiently increased to form a town.

The main commercial street was Sheep Street, later to be renamed Woodfield Street. The first places of worship to be built were Libanus at Market Street in 1772 and St John's church (the church in the middle of the road) in 1789. One of the oldest public houses that became yet another victim to bulldozers in the 1960s was the Welcome-to-Town at Woodfield Street, as did The Bush Inn (now the Wychtree Underpass). The area south of Morris' Town became home to tinplate manufacturers such as Upper Forest & Worcester, Dyffryn, Midland & Tircanol and Beaufort. These works are no longer in existence, having all closed in the 1950s-'60s, and being redeveloped into the Swansea Enterprise Park in the 1980s.

Morriston once boasted almost a public house to every place of worship; however our churches and chapels are very few today. We once had Horeb (1842), Calfaria (1878); Nazareth (1898) and Glantawe Methodist, all of which are no longer in existence.

Morriston boasts the housing of the Driving Vehicle Licensing Agency at Clase, a large hospital at Maes Y Gwernen and a choir recognized as one of the finest in the world – the Morriston Orpheus Male Voice Choir – founded by the late Mr Ivor Sims. Morriston has as much history in its people as its buildings. It has been people such as these that have helped Morriston to develop into the town it has become. Newcomers are welcomed but need to remember that Morriston has to be preserved and cared for.

Today, a walk along Woodfield Street highlights the changes in our social behaviour as much as the commercial alterations. The high volume of traffic is a complete comparison to the lack of quality shops. It is a shame to see Woodfield Street not reaching the high standards it used to meet twenty years ago but this is progress.

Clasemont House, 1760.

As the years pass more people will view this book as an historical database – to learn about the past. I hope you enjoy looking back at the good old days of Morriston and join me in a celebration of fifteen years of writing books on this interesting and deeply historical town – Morriston.

One
1890s-1940s

A Morriston wedding in 1897. A rare photograph of a wedding group after their marriage ceremony at Libanus chapel in Market Street.

ORDER OF SERVICE

HELD BY THE

NONCONFORMISTS OF MORRISTON

AT THE

TABERNACLE CHAPEL

In Memory of our Late Great

MONARCH

QUEEN VICTORIA,

ON

The Day of Her Majesty's Funeral,

2nd FEBRUARY, 1901.

Chairman - Rev. W. EMLYN JONES.

Organist - Mrs. T. J. DAVIES.

Musical Conductor, Mr. W. PENFRO ROWLANDS.

MORRISTON & CLYDACH :

JONES & SONS, STEAM PRINTERS, BOOKBINDERS, &c.

Poster showing the order of service at Tabernacle chapel to mourn the passing of Queen Victoria.

A unique view of Woodfield Street and the surrounding area in 1902 from the top of St John's church tower.

The non-commercial end of Woodfield Street in 1904 with its long gardens and trees. It is difficult to imagine Sheep Street as a residential street but it was the foundation of the original grid layout in the late 1700s.

A celebration for the Coronation of Kind Edward VII in August 1902 at Dillwyn Street (later renamed Glantawe Street after Lord Glantawe, J.J. Jenkins, who owned the Beaufort Tinplate Works).

A rare view over the village of Pentrepoeth and F.W. Burkes' Chemical Works in 1909.

In 1903 Charles Wilkins, a visitor to the Upper Forest Tinplate Works, wrote: 'Such was the idea presented by one face of a thoughtful worker. This girl-woman had a leather apron and two leather gloves, and the ease with which she seized upon a plate, struck it a blow, and ripped it into sheets, was wonderful. Layer after layer came off just like stripping one vegetable layer from another, instead of tough steel.'

The men at Upper Forest Tinplate Works in 1902. Working conditions were grim compared to today's standards. A retired employee of the Upper Forest Works states, 'Tin sheets would fly out at all unexpected angles, causing cuts to the bone time and time again. Gashes were only considered 'officially,' if the blood was spoiling the tin-sheets, otherwise first-aid consisted of slapping a dollop of warm grease on the cut and wrapping it in sacking. Even the greasers were envied if they were able to go to the toilet in the normal working hours. This was called a high life.'

William Treharne's sweet shop in December 1906, situated on the corner of Crown Street and Woodfield Street.

The ladies of St David's church in 1915.

Tirpenry Street children in 1917.

Women of Tircanol Works in the 1920s. It has been said that the skill of women operating the slitting machines in the past was unsurpassed by males. Women were also engaged in the pickling departments and worked alongside boys and young men in the cold rolls sections.

A rare photograph taken in 1920 of the floats at Woodfield Street during the original-style Morriston Carnival.

This unique photograph depicts all the children who were in attendance at Cwmrhydyceirw school when it opened in 1923.

A class from Neath Road Senior girl's school in 1928.

Clasemont Road prior to road widening in 1929.

Clasemont Road after road widening in 1930.

The cross-section of Pentrepoeth Road and Springfield Street in 1929 compared with a year later (below), when road widening had caused a dramatic and pleasant change to the area.

Pentrepoeth/ Springfield in 1930.

As a result of road widening, this was Pentrepoeth Road (the hill) in 1931. The only focal point is the old vicarage in the background of the photograph. Below is Clasemont Road, taken at the same time. Today, detached and semi-detached houses dominate the landscape.

Clasemont Road 1931. A class photograph of Cwmrhydyceirw Infant's school in 1933.

A class photograph of Cwmrhydyceirw Infant's school in 1933.

Graig Infant's school class in 1934.

An Ebenezer chapel group photograph which was taken in the 1930s. Ebenezer was situated on Cwmrhydyceirw Road.

This rare photograph shows the construction of new houses at Heol Tir Du, Cwmrhydyceirw, in the 1930s.

Left: Regal Cinema owner Alec Hyman arranged day trips for the children of the unemployed during the 'Hungry 1930s'. *Right:* Alex Hyman in the 1930s.

This very rare snap was taken of the children who attended these outings. They had never seen the seaside and it was thanks to fundraising activities that a picnic and free transport were provided. Difficult times were made easier by the people of Morriston working together under the direction of Mr Alec Hyman, known to this generation of children as 'Uncle Alex'.

Staff of Dora Café in 1939. The premises of Dora Café is today an estate agents in Woodfield Street whose basement is used by a taxi firm.

Teachers gather the brothers and sisters of Neath Road Infant's school for a photograph in the late 1930s.

The Singing Company (Young People's Choir) of the Morriston Salvation Army Corps in 1938.

Class photograph from 1937 of Martin Street boy's school. The school was demolished in 1991 and St Martin's residential home now stands on its site.

Morriston Home Guard at Pentrepoeth playing fields in 1942.

Ebenezer chapel, Cwmrhydyceirw. Performers of *Agatha* pose for a photograph in 1944. Almost sixty years later and now the chapel is for sale – probably to be demolished.

A wonderful image of a man stoking the furnace at Swansea Vale Works in 1944.

Retired gentlemen gather outside William Treharne's sweet shop on Woodfield Street in 1944. The Welcome-to-Town public house and Regal Cinema can be seen in the background.

A rare photograph of a United States Forces Club Dance at Libanus chapel vestry in 1944.

The Morriston Orpheus Male Voice Choir pictured here at the corner of Clase Road and Glantawe Street in 1947 after becoming National Winners at Colwyn Bay.

A photograph of the Upper Forest Tinplate Works cricket team taken at Morriston Park in 1948. Note in the background are the swimming baths and Llwyneryr House – both recently demolished.

The true reality of washing day within a backyard at Neath Road towards the end of the Second World War.

Two
1950s-1960s

Children of Bath Road.

Nurses presenting gifts to patients at Morriston Hospital in the 1950s.

Prize-giving at Tabernacle chapel.

Woodfield Street in the 1950s, where you could purchase almost anything. Morriston boasted an excellent shopping centre where many people – not only those living in Morriston – would shop.

A wonderful composition showing a narrow view of Clyndu Street in the 1950s, prior to demolition to widen the road. Behind the bus is the Old Prince public house, which is still in business today.

The Young People's Guild of Aenon Baptist chapel, Strawberry Place, gather together for a photograph in 1955.

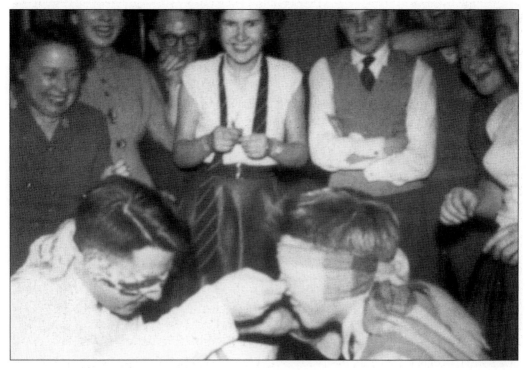

Aenon chapel's young people holding a Christmas party in 1955.

The Singing Company of the Salvation Army in the 1950s, conducted by Mrs Nancy Lear.

The Songster Brigade also from the 1950s, conducted by Mr Eric Lear. The service both Nancy and Eric have given the Salvation Army at Morriston is commendable.

Some of the staff of Hopkin Morgan Bakery, Lower Morfydd Street, in October 1952, taken in the office. Hopkin Morgan Bakery became a Mother's Pride Bakery, which is today the room at the top function room.

The people of Crown Street (ideally named on such an occasion) celebrate the Coronation of Queen Elizabeth II by holding a party in June 1953.

The Morriston Orpheus in London in 1956. Front row, from left to right: Mr and Mrs Tommy Elias, Mr Ivor Sims, Mrs Greta Sims, Morriston bookmaker, Mr Billy Williams.

A wonderful photograph of Mr Ivor Sims in 1956, conducting the choir that he founded – The Morriston Orpheus Male Voice Choir – during a rehearsal at the parish hall.

Staff of John Bull General Store in 1958 . The site of this shop is now occupied by a Kwik-Save supermarket.

Hard to recognise this view today, but the two most prominent buildings in the photograph are now the Wychtree Underpass. This was Clase Road in 1953. Behind the Nag's Head on the left is the UNO Tinplate Containers, now Castle Bingo.

Store 294 of Boots the Chemist, at the top of Woodfield Street in 1960. If you look carefully you may see the photographer via the reflection in the glass. This building is today Idris William's Hitachi shop.

Woodfield Street in 1960. Five years later would see the Regal Cinema and various shops on the left of the photograph demolished to make way for 'modern' shops with hardly an architectural feature, except for a square design with extra pavement.

A view of Wychtree Bridge and Bush Inn, now the site of the Wychtree Underpass. The chimneys on the right stand alongside the Upper Forest and Worcester Tinplate Works. Today the site is an Asda hypermarket.

An extremely rare birds-eye view of Swansea Vale Spelter Works in 1962. To provide you with a current landmark, the church of St Samlet can be seen in the background towards the left.

The members of the Salvation Army photographed at Blackpool in the early 1960s.

A unique photograph taken from the roof of Tabernacle chapel in 1962. Clearly seen is the cleared site of the Forest and Worcester Tinplate Works, the land later bought by Morganite. The Dyffryn Tinplate Works was still in operation when this photograph was taken. The Enterprise Park had yet to be built.

Another similar photograph taken at the same time of Woodfield Street and Pentrepoeth. If you look carefully you might see the bronze statue of Mercury on the dome of the Regal Cinema.

Only recently this unique 1962 photograph and the one below were discovered in glorious colour. The photographer stands on Graig Road and captures the top of Clyndu Street. In the background is the house that stood on the corner of Tan-y-Lan and Lan Street for many years. It sadly caught fire and was demolished in 2002.

No, it's not a scene from the Yorkshire Dales, but the top of Clyndu Street before being demolished to widen the road. The Old Prince Inn is an ideal focal point.

Tan-y-lan cottages.

Many of the houses and cottages on Clyndu Street were demolished due to extensive road widening in the late 1960s, including the cottage seen on the right. However, the cottages (above) alongside Graig Infant's school survived, but are now much altered.

The ladies of Morriston Golf Club attend a dinner at the Langland Bay Hotel in 1962.

Half of Morriston Orpheus Choir outside Swansea railway station in the 1960s.

The male members of the Gilbert and Sullivan Operatic Group of St David's church in September 1966, performing *The Gondoliers*. From left to right: Gwyn Lewis, John Christopher, Ian Thomas, Alwyn Chant, Stan Hope, David Evans, Revd Clifford Knight, Adrian Uren.

The ladies of the same performance. Back row, from left to right: Betty Geary, Megan Hill, Jean Burgess, Olwen Chant, Elaine Hope, Glenys Tanner, Ann Craven, Hazel Davies, Nan Morris. Front row, from left to right: Anne Llewellyn, Betty Jenkins, Eulonwy Loosemore, Linda Llewellyn, Avril Hughes.

The members of the St David's church Gilbert and Sullivan Operatic Group in 1969. The conductor in the centre of the photograph is Revd Hubert Hughes. The accompanist Lily Bowden Watts is situated on the left in the front of the photograph.

A final photograph of the operatic group at the parish hall where rehearsals and production would take place. From left to right: Philip Thomas, Ian Thomas, Stan Hope, Tony Holt, David Morris, Stan Chant, Mary Phillips, Elved Rees, John Christopher, Revd Gordon Morris, Lily Bowden Watts, Cyril Scott, Gareth Matthews, Alwyn Chant.

Two photographs, above and opposite, that barely capture the event that took Morriston by storm. Crowds await the arrival of the new Prince of Wales, His Royal Highness Prince Charles, in 1969.

Crowds outside Tabernacle chapel in 1969.

These fortunate children might well have caught a glimpse of Prince Charles in 1969. The photograph was taken in the lower yard of Martin Street boy's school.

HARRY'S STORES

Morriston's SPAR Foodliner

LIBBY'S PEACHES A1.T. **1/7**	LIBBY'S PEARS A1.T. **1/9**	Crosse & Blackwell Ham/Chicken Roll Ham/Beef Roll **1/6**	INFLATABLE BEACH BALLS ONLY **1/11 ea.**	CHEF BEANS/ SAUSAGE **1/-**
VIOTA FRENCH SANDWICH Vanilla, Coffee, Lemon **1/4**	LIBBY'S RED SALMON **3/11**	DIXCEL TOILET ROLLS **1/4**	LIFEGUARD DISINFECTANT GIANT **2/-**	MARY BAKER VANILLA DELIGHTS Orange Supremes **11d.**

KARDOV FLOUR PLAIN S.R. **3lb. - 1/9**	OVEN READY **ROSS CHICKENS** 2lb. 12oz. **8/6** 3lb. 10oz. **11/9** 4lb. 4oz. **14/-** plus FREE ½lb. Pkt. BIRDS EYE PEAS	LIBBY'S CREAMED PUDDINGS RICE MACARONI **10d.**
ROBINSON'S WHOLE ORANGE/LEMON only **1/11**		LIBBY'S CORNED BEEF 7oz **2/9** 12oz. **4/3**

PROVISION DEPARTMENT Bowyers Beef & Pork Sausage (8s) **6**d. OFF per lb.	WINES AND SPIRITS DEPARTMENT **CINZANO BIANCO** RED BIANCO DRY **21/-**	COMMANDERIE ST. JOHN CYPRUS WINE **10/- bott.**
FRUIT & VEGETABLE DEPARTMENT JONATHAN EATING APPLES **1/6** per lb.	Collect a form showing Reduced Price Offers when purchasing a bottle	

OFF LICENCE DEPARTMENT OPEN AT NORMAL SHOP HOURS
MONDAY 12.30 - 5.20 (Half Day). TUESDAY & WEDNESDAY 9.00 - 5.20. THURSDAY 9.00 - 6.00. FRIDAY 9.00 - 7.45 (Late Night). SATURDAY 9.00 - 1.00 (Half Day)

A 1969 advertisement for Harry's Stores at Clase Road.

Three
1970s-Present Day

A Martin Street school class photograph taken in 1971.

The following four photographs show the opening ceremony of Morriston M4 junction and bypass at Ynysforgan on the 16 September 1972.

Local councillor Mr John Allison speaks on this special occasion.

The unveiling ceremony of a plaque to mark the event by The Rt Hon. Peter Thomas QC, MP, Secretary of State for Wales.

Standing beside the commemorative stone and plaque is local businessman Mr J.P. Williams and his wife.

These photographs were taken in November 1974 during the final days of the Forward Movement Hall at Woodfield Street. The site was purchased by Tesco Stores Ltd and used to extend the premises seen here.

It is hard to imagine now that there was a much-loved musical venue in between these modern buildings. Note the car in the window of Tesco!

This was the view from the doorway of the Forward Movement Hall a few days prior to demolition.

View looking up Woodfield Street from the outer wall of the Forward Movement Hall in November 1974.

An old Morriston family business – Hunt's Bakers – situated at No. 52 Woodfield Street. Seen here in the mid-1970s are the family of Mr and Mrs Hunt, seemingly in solemn mood. The building was later sold to Charles Sayer and is now Morriston Job Centre.

A view of Woodfield Street in 1976 during a parade of the Morriston Millitares.

They continued marching through Woodfield Street and past Bethania chapel, which celebrated its 100th anniversary two years later in 1978.

Marching at Morriston Cross in 1976, past Pompa's café and the original premises of Alan Hole Newsagents, which moved in 1988 to its present location under the name Good News Newsagents. Note the Guards cigarette machine on the wall.

Morriston Songsters of the Salvation Army photographed in September 1977 for a tour of Sweden. Seated in the centre is songster leader Mr Eric Lear.

Celebrations were in full swing in June 1977 when Peter Davies with son Andrew and Anne Lewis with André Scoville (aged five years) were photographed at Pentremalwed Road celebrating the Queen's Silver Jubilee.

Graig Infant's school, class two in 1977. Class teacher on the left is Mrs Ranft and she is accompanied on the right by the headmistress, Miss Hartnell.

Class four of Graig Infant's school in 1979. Headmistress on the left is Miss Hartnell and the class teacher is Mrs Vaughan.

The Smelter's Arms at Trewyddfa Road in June 1980. Originally built in 1821 and rebuilt in 1921, this building is – as it appears here – boarded up. Today this junction with Graig Road has traffic lights to assist with calming measures for a road that wasn't meant for heavy traffic.

This was the original Wychtree roundabout in 1980. This area of Morriston was much altered in 1994 with the opening of the Wychtree underpass. Note the abandoned buildings of the Dyffryn Tinplate Works on the right of the photograph, which have since been demolished.

Class 1B of Bishop Vaughan Comprehensive school in 1980.

The staff of Morriston Senior Comprehensive school in 1980.

The staff and pupils of Pentrepoeth Infant's school, celebrating 100 years in 1981.

Pentrepoeth school staff pose for a photograph to celebrate the school's centenary in 1981.

The staff of the Supasnaps photographic shop in Woodfield Street in 1982, during the Morriston Shopping Festival week in which staff from many Morriston shops dressed in attire from the early 1900s.

Staff at the Welsh Pantry bakers and confectioners at Pentrepoeth Road line up for their photograph in 1982.

The blizzard of 1982 brought Morriston to a standstill. Schools were closed, and therefore all the children could be seen on make-do sleighs. As seen here, the snow was thick and roadways were the safest places to walk.

Morriston Cross with not a car in sight.

The bottom of Pentrepoeth Road during the blizzard of 1982.

Pentrepoeth Road at the entrance of what was at the time of this image Pentrepoeth Farm in 1982.

Woodfield Street on a wet weekday in 1984 prior to Tesco moving to the newly created Swansea Enterprise Park.

Morriston Cross in the summer of 1984, when the intersection of roads were uncomplicated and easy to cross.

The exterior of Tabernacle schoolroom on Trewyddfa Road. It had its foundation stone laid by Alderman William Thomas of Lan in 1883 and it stood here until its unnoticed demolition in 2001 – a total of 118 years.

This was the interior of the disused schoolroom in 1985 after vandals had broken in and wrote graffiti on the walls. It was once home to Sunday school children and didn't deserve such disrespectful treatment.

These photographs were taken during the two-hundredth anniversary of St John's church (the church in the middle of the road) in May 1989 from the top of the tower. Clearly depicted here is Woodfield Street with the tower of Tabernacle standing very proudly. Compare the same view taken eighty-seven years ago on page 11.

View of Martin Street from the tower in 1989. Note the vacated junior boys' school awaiting its fate on the right.

View of the original Morganite site, which is today Asda hypermarket and Brewster's restaurant. The site of the UNO Tinplate Containers had been demolished – later Castle Bingo was to be constructed on the land.

The Bevan's Arms on the corner of Morfydd Street in May 1989. At the time, houses were being demolished at Pentremalwed Road and at Graig Terrace.

Martin Street Boys' school during demolition in May 1991 ended a remarkable era of history. Although the building seen here achieved more than 120 years as a teaching establishment, two previous schools had occupied the site, thus totalling 176 years.

An hour after this image was recorded, the school hall was demolished. Many assemblies were held here along with class photographs.

The final few minutes of two classrooms that looked out onto Martin Street in May 1991.

The demolition of the last section of Martin Street school in 1991. St Martin's Residential Home stands on both the school site and yard today, having been built in 1993.

Ladies of the Salvation Army in 1990.

In early 1992 the Salvation Army at Morfydd Street was completely renovated and reopened by Councillor John Allison.

In 1994 a discount store occupied the premises previously known as Wilding's at No. 103 Woodfield Street.

Morriston Cross had a change of image in 1994 when the 153-year-old pub had its name changed from the Cross Inn to the Rat and Carrot. However, the change didn't last for long and it was renamed The Cross Inn.

Prior to reaching the hustle and bustle of Wychtree roundabout, this was the scene at Neath Road in March 1994 and before the construction of the Wychtree underpass.

Only three months later, Neath Road was in the midst of construction and it was hard to imagine what it would look like when completed.

In the summer of 1996 the contractor Edmund Nuttall Ltd thanked residents of Morriston by organizing a concert underneath the underpass featuring the Accordian Band and Morriston Orpheus Choir. This was an occasion never to be repeated again.

The Wychtree underpass – officially opened in November 1996 – is pictured here in March 1999.

Construction of Asda hypermarket in March 1999. The photograph was taken from the vacant site of the Dyffryn Tinplate Works.

The vacant land in March 1999 which Burger King and Kentucky Fried Chicken now occupy. This was land that Morganite once dominated and previously the Forest and Worcester Tinplate Works owned.

The corner of Lan Street and Tan-y-Lan in 2000. The corner house caught fire and was demolished recently, changing the landscape and the history of this area.

The last remaining days of the London Hosiery shop at No. 25 Woodfield Street in April 2000.

Obviously taken on a Sunday, this was Woodfield Street in July 2000. Note the zebra crossing has moved further down.

The pelican crossing has also moved from outside Woolworth's to St David's church.

Four

Down Memory Lane

Morriston Cross in 1933 after road widening had taken place.

Situated on the corner of Morfydd Street and Woodfield Street is the Bevans Arms. It is pictured here in 1974.

The Bevans Arms in 1988.

Taken during the construction of Morganite in the 1960s. Today the majority of the site is occupied by an Asda store, Brewster's restaurant and a Travel Inn.

This 1960s photograph depicts the drainage operation of the Swansea Canal. Neath Road looks very different today. (See pages 74 and 75).

Although the name of Bath Villa lives on in the form of a cul-de-sac, the original Bath Villa was once a large house owned by the proprietor of the Beaufort Tinplate Works, Morgan E. Rees.

The Morriston Orpheus Male Voice Choir is photographed at Bath Villa in 1946 after winning the National Eisteddfod at Mountain Ash. Seated in the centre on the left of the cup is the founder of the choir, Mr Ivor Sims, and the choir accompanist Miss Lillian Abbott is seated last but one on the left in the front row.

Philadelphia Welsh Calvinistic Methodist chapel celebrated its 200th anniversary in 2002, but now its future is very much undecided. The original chapel was built in 1802 on land owned by relations of the Morris family (John Morris). The rent was one peppercorn per annum!

Although the exterior was plastered in 1935, the chapel has remained the same since this building was built in 1829 on the site of the old building. It is such an achievement for the chapel to reach this remarkable milestone considering how very few members Philadelphia now has. It is almost as old as Morriston itself but is a forgotten landmark.

Opposite, top: Interior of the Tabernacle chapel showing original organ in 1914.

Opposite, bottom: This photograph was taken in 1986 and shows the current organ which celebrates its eightieth anniversary in 2002. The stained-glass windows were also placed there in 1922.

Above: Wooden scaffolding, wooden ladders, a strong religious faith and superb skills of craftsmanship are what these men in this photograph had to work with. Throughout 1869–1872 they built a 'cathedral of non-conformity' to be proud of. Their sweat and toil made it more their chapel than that of the élite chapel members that were to worship there.

*Right:*This magnificent building named New Libanus was opened in December 1872, built in this way to clearly depict the wealth of its worshippers due to important tinplate owners and gentry forming the original committee. Tabernacle, as it was later called, celebrates its 130th anniversary in December 2002.

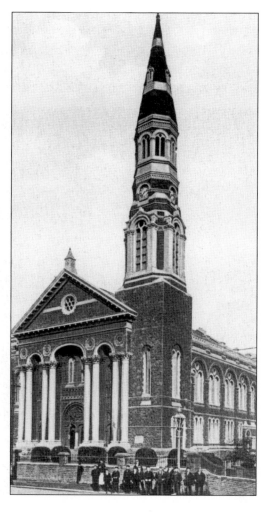

Tabernacle continuing to dominate the landscape as pictured here in 1956.

Cyril Cooke Ltd premises, within the old ticket office of Morriston railway station, photographed here in the 1970s.

Cyril Cooke Ltd Wesleyan chapel. Later the business moved to the then vacant Wesleyan English Methodist church at Glantawe Street. During 2001 the business ceased operating, and the site was sold. Residential buildings are now on the site.

The staff of the original Charles Sayers shop at 52 Woodfield Street (now Morriston Job Centre) in 1953. The lady dressed in black is Mrs Griffiths, known as 'Mrs G'. She is standing by Margaret Cornelius.

In the late 1990s, Charles Sayers' daughter reopened the business at its new location, 103 Woodfield Street, where Wildings had traded for many years. This photograph was taken in July 1999.

St John's church in 1960. Originally built in wood in 1789, it was rebuilt in 1857; the towers were added later.

The interior of St John's church in 1984. Recently, the Church of Wales sold the building to the Ragamuffin group, who teach performing arts to underprivileged children. We must hope that St John's church isn't allowed to decay but is used to enhance our town and people.

Times they are a changing! The familiar business name of Uriel Rees, Ironmongers, had closed down and trees seem to dominate the upper end of Woodfield Street here in 1974.

This photograph was taken from the corner of Martin Street and Morfydd Street in 1974. Note the side door of the Bevans Arms, altered to become a window. The public conveniences at Woodfield Street had yet to be built.

Another view of Woodfield Street in 1974 from outside the Powells Arms (now called Champion Brewers).

Part of St John's church, the Bevans Arms and the vacant premises of Uriel Rees, Iron-mongers, in 1974.

This 1875 police station was converted during the Second World War to become an auxiliary fire station in addition to the police station. It is one of very few nineteenth-century buildings that remain standing.

Left: Sway Road fire station in 1983. *Right:* The new fire headquarters for West Glamorgan was built on the site of the old fire station at Sway Road.

The staff of Lipton line up outside the shop for a photograph in 1930.

This photograph was taken during the Morriston Shopping Festival, which took place in 1981.

The men of the Midland Tinplate Works in the 1920s.

A decade later sees the women and girls of the Midland Tinplate Works, with the 'gaffer' sitting on the right of the photograph.

Women meeting their husbands on pay day at the Morriston Midland Tinplate Works in the 1920s. The photograph was taken from the Tircanol side, looking towards the Wychtree Bridge direction.

This was the Midland (& Tircanol) Tinplate Works prior to demolition in 1987, taken from Bush Road. On its site today is DFS Furniture Store.

People who have moved to Morriston or who have been born within the last ten years would be forgiven for not knowing how much Pentremalwed Road has changed. This was Pentremalwed Road taken at the junction with Clyndu Street in April 1986.

The houses that exist at Pentremalwed Road today are unaffected by the devastation that arose during 1988-1989. This photograph shows the gutted houses of 74 to 71 Pentremalwed Road, prior to demolition. Generations of families had lived here for decades but, due to a landslide, the inevitable had to happen.

August 1989 saw the demolition of these four red-bricked houses. It was a tremendously sad time having to watch a neighbourhood be torn apart in this way. Also affected were Plas-y-Coed Road, Plas-y-Coed Terrace, Graig Terrace and Glan Terrace, all of which are now but a distant memory. The council must take action to avoid the same thing happening to a small section of Trewyddfa Road, which is also crumbling away.

The road in 1994, looking vastly different. Today, the view is worse, with wild trees growing high on the site that was once home to a much-loved neighbourhood. Fortunately, Pentremalwed House on the right of this photograph and the remaining houses that stand at Pentremalwed Road today are unaffected by the landslide.

Martin Street with Martin Street boy's school and Pokers Row in 1929. When the rent man came to call, each neighbour would bang the party wall with a poker to warn of his arrival!

The same scene in 1988 when Lloyds Terrace, as it was officially but not often called, was demolished in the 1960s to be constructed as a large yard of the adjacent boys' school. The school closed its doors after 173 years when it merged with Pentrepoeth girl's school.

The schoolyard at Martin Street, prior to its being churned up when the school was demolished in 1991.

April 1993 saw the first private forty-bedroomed residential home of St Martin's Court, built on the site of the schoolyard. Shortly after, the site of the school was used to build another forty bedroomed home. The cobbled ramp used by many hundreds of thousands of children through the years, which joined the top yard to the school, was a feature kept by the owners of the home.

Staff of Hunts Bakers, Woodfield Street.

Turbaned ladies of Hunts Bakers.

The bakery staff of a Morriston family business, Hunts Bakers & Confectioners, which were situated at 52-54 Woodfield Street (now Morriston Job Centre). These photographs were taken in around 1949.

The manager of the Upper Forest & Worcester Tinplate Works, holding a memorial service in 1918 for the men who once worked at the works but who were killed during the First World War.

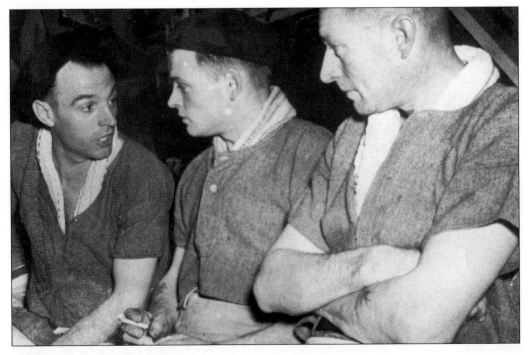

Three men photographed before their shift commenced at the Upper Forest & Worcester Tinplate Works in the 1930s. An Asda, a Burger King, a KFC, Brewster restaurant and Morganite now occupy the site of the works.

Woodfield Street in the 1920s. The building in the background towards the left of the tram was Hunts Bakers & Confectioners. The buildings on the immediate left were demolished in the 1960s, when Tesco built its store on the site.

The manager (right) and staff of the Co-operative Society Shop, known as the Co-op, situated at Clase Road in 1931. The registered office of the Co-op in Swansea was at Gower Street (later renamed The Kingsway).

The members of Morriston's Hanney's Band, photographed at Morriston Park bandstand in the late 1920s.

Morriston tennis team, photographed at Morriston Park, in 1939.

Here is a photograph of Class 1A of Graig school at Tan-y-Lan, in 1923.

Leonard Vagg (right) was photographed to advertise Fry's Chocolate and Cocoa during the First World War.

The first choir of St David's church in 1891, photographed at the vicarage at Pentrepoeth.

Morriston Hockey Team in 1927.

Teachers of Neath Road school in 1937. From left to right: Eluned Harris, Joan Conibear, Winnie Thomas, Miriam Williams, Miss Rees, Freda Rees and Maggie B. Jones.

The Chemical Road detachment of the brave ARP Wardens (Air-Raid Precaution) pose for a photograph in around 1944.

June 1973 saw BBC television's *Blue Peter* presenter John Noakes as the guest of Morriston Carnival. After the procession through Morriston the carnival would continue in the grounds of Morriston Hospital; in those days the hospital was a quarter of the size that it is today.

Morriston carnivals were notorious throughout Swansea for being the best. Other celebrities to grace our streets have been Diana Dors, Gareth Hunt, Paul Henry (Benny from *Crossroads*) and John Craven.

A hot summer day in June 1978 at Woodfield Street. The famous guest star was Anne Kirkbride, better known to everyone at that time as Deirdre Langton (now Barlow/Rachid) in *Coronation Street*.

Other stars from *Coronation Street* to have visited Morriston include Peter Adamson (Len Fairclough), Pat Phoenix (Elsie Tanner), and Geoffrey Hughes (Eddie Yates).

Marching bands and large crowds are remembered of those gloriously warm days of Morriston carnivals.

1980 saw the visit of ATV's *Tiswas* host, Sally James.

A Morriston carnival float in the mid-1980s. Throughout the late 1980s, the ground at Morriston Hospital was becoming increasingly difficult to house the carnival owing to the quantity of medical buildings being built.

For the past couple of years the Rotary Club of Morriston have held a smaller scale Morriston Carnival.

A charming photograph of Clydach Road on 6 February 1925. Parallel to the uniformed chimneys is the railway line and canal (alongside the railings).

Clydach Road, in the mid-1970s, prior to the construction of the massive Ynysforgan roundabout that exists today. Today, Clydach Road has traffic cameras enforcing the speed limit.

Morriston Star Laundry at Bush Road in the 1950s, now the site of McDonalds and Matalan.

This was the view of the Wychtree roundabout in September 1982. Clearly visible are the buildings of the UNO Tinplate Containers Ltd, which were demolished in 1986, now the site of Castle Bingo.

The entrance gates to Pentrepoeth House at Pentrepoeth Road in 1929. Notice how narrow the road is in this photograph.

The same view in 1932 after a road-widening scheme had been completed. A considerable amount of trees belonging to Pentrepoeth House were lost in widening the road.

Martin Street in 1928, prior to clearing away rubble caused by half-demolished houses.

Martin Street in March 1931, photographed from the same location but now looking a great deal better.

This photograph was taken when a train entered Morriston railway station for the final time before closing. The photograph is taken in the direction of Clase Road.

The abandoned platform, photographed here in October 1982, from the bridge at Clase Road.

A car park called Morriston Park and Ride was developed in 1986 on the site of the railway platform and track, but was hardly ever used.

Today the site has been developed into a housing estate and a large car park for customers of Castle Bingo Hall (built on the site of the former UNO Tinplate Containers Ltd). The current West & Wales train service incorporates the use of small local stations, including Llansamlet and Skewen, whereas if insight had been used, Morriston railway line would have been a wonderful way of easing congestion of traffic within our town.

General view over Morriston, *c.* 1870. Clearly visible is St John's church, and also the Clyndu Pit (in the bottom left side of this photograph). It extended as far as Llangyfelach and Upper Clase Farm, and worked under what is now Morriston cemetery and crematorium. The colliery closed in 1841. In the background on the right is Swansea Vale Spelter Works, which closed in the 1870s.

A charming photograph, taken on 6 March 1931 at Woodfield Street. Swansea United billposting company are in the process of changing the cinema advertisements for both the Gem and the Regal. Long may the building of St John's church remain on this sacred site.

Five
How it all Began

Growing up throughout the 1970s, I would often ask both my parents and my maternal grandparents if there were any books on the history of Morriston. Their reply was always the same: 'No, but why don't you write one André and be the first?' Fifteen years on and four books later, I'm now closing my fifth book (my fourth on Morriston) with a chapter on the people that have influenced me and some photographs that give an insight into my life so far. In writing my first book, entitled *Morriston's Pictorial Past*, I met with many difficult challenges, including the gaining of peoples' trust when asking to borrow photographs. They would often be reluctant, as they had never heard of me and weren't sure if they would ever see them again. However, at the age of fourteen years I started writing the book and was fortunate enough to watch it rolling off the press two years later, surrounded by reporters and photographers from *The Western Mail* and *South Wales Evening Post* newspapers. It was a proud moment and a dream come true.

I was born on 16 November 1972, and for nine years I lived here at Pentremalwed House with my parents Joan and Denzil, although they lived at Pentremalwed Road for many years before I was born. To see how much this area has changed saddens me, especially when I remember how happy we were living in such a lovely neighbourhood.

My dad and I photographed walking along the now unrecognisable part of Pentremalwed Road, in May 1974. I dedicated my second book to two people who I will never forget, our next door neighbour, the late Mrs Ellen Williams (Auntie Williams) and her sister Mrs Margaret Lowe (Auntie Maggie). They both feature very much in my childhood and I have never forgotten them.

My mum and I returning home from Morriston Carnival. The photograph was taken at Morfydd Street in 1975. I can clearly remember the older gentlemen sitting on a seat at the 'Wac' (now overgrown) and listening to the brass-band music coming from our radiogram. It was a beautiful hot summer's day in the mid-1970s, and the men would shout up to my dad Denzil, 'Turn it up Denz!'. They were good days.

The mid-1970s, and the flared trousers were in fashion for the first time when this photograph was taken. I am standing outside my home at Pentremalwed House before going to Sunday school at the Salvation Army Citadel. I don't wear such clothes today.

My late maternal grandparents, Elsie May and David John Gower, pictured on the occasion of their sixtieth wedding anniversary in 1980. They were both born in the last decade of the nineteenth century, and lived for the majority of their lives in Morriston. I would visit them almost every day and sit in between them and ask them to tell me about 'old' Morriston; of course to them, the 'old' Morriston was so clear in their memories that they would paint such a vivid picture I thought I was there. Although my grandmother never lived to see my books, I know she would have been as proud as my grandfather was. We all miss them so much but I know they're always with me now. Grandparents are so special and these were no exception.

I am photographed here on 15 June 1974 (at the age of eighteen months) in the arms of my uncle, the late Iorwerth Lewis (1927 – 1988) at Morriston Carnival. I never missed attending the carnivals, and meeting Uncle Iorwerth was an added treat. Faces would light up when he met them, due to his liking of people and his practical jokes.

A wonderful photograph of Uncle Iorwerth in 1986 trying on a bowler hat at Carm Market. I can still recall the delight in his face when he grabbed the arm of my mu (left), and when Auntie Mary, his wife (centre), walked away saying 'Not again, courageously fought the pain of motor-neurone disease, but after a long fight passe 27 July 1988 at the age of sixty-one years. His funeral procession allowed him to final time through Morriston and it was during this time, when I saw Morriston absolute standstill, I realised we had lost someone very special. He lives, as he ha in our hearts forever.

I was photographed in 1979, when Swansea pantomime star Kenny Smiles visited Mr Bill Mead's (left) music shop, Mead Music, High Street, Swansea. I started playing the organ at the age of six years. I later progressed into playing semi-professionally, and then became self employed. I have been fortunate enough to play keyboards for Her Royal Highness the Duchess of York, Ruth Madoc and Emlyn Hughes.

rthen
, Joan
or!'. He
away on
ass for the
come to an
always done,

ard that I had a vast collection of old picture postcards
t me. My parents used to visit antique stalls and buy
a time when they were quite expensive. This was the only
ne to see. My Morriston postcards are a collection that means
y parents so much.

Morgan Tonen and I, photographed in August 1986. I first met Mr Tonen in 1985 when I purchased some photographs from him. We kept in touch and because we both had a strong passion for local history he broadened my interests, to include presenting slide-shows, photography, darkroom techniques and learning Welsh. He became a large influence in my life during this time. He suddenly passed away in 1987 aged seventy, and therefore never saw my books. I was fortunate to have known him and to have learned so much from such a kind-hearted man.

I did it! One month after my sixteenth birthday and I am photographed here with the sta[ff] the newly-opened Good News Newsagent during a busy book signing on a Saturday mo[r] in December 1988. Morriston's first book, entitled *Morriston's Pictorial Past*, went on s[ale] the 1 December 1988 and sold over 3,000 copies. It was reprinted a year before Volu[me] was published in 1994. Although both books are now out of print, *Morriston Then &* published in 1999 by Tempus Publishing. It featured the majority of the 'old' photogr[aphs] my archives, and the 'new' photographs, were taken by local photographer, Jeff La[ ] Swansea (my first book on Swansea) was published in 2000, featuring a chapter o[ ] and again published by Tempus.

Two people that have stood by me throughout my life have been my parents Joan and Denzil. They are photographed (above) during my book signing in December 1988. Denzil became the youngest person to start work at Swansea Vale Works and the youngest to become foreman. He later worked for CEGB/ National Grid where he took early retirement in 1996. Joan worked for many years at Marks & Spencer, Swansea, before taking early retirement in 2001. They celebrate their thirty-ninth wedding anniversary in 2003.

This photograph was taken at Pendine in June 1974. When I began writing my first book at the age of fourteen, I never dreamed that I would be writing my fifth book all these years later. I achieved my ambition of writing the first book on Morriston and for bringing memories of nostalgia into the lives of thousands of Morristonians all over the world. I have discovered that all you need in life are people to support and love you – and if you have a dream you can make it come true.

Now, in my thirtieth year, I look forward to what lies ahead; although Morriston has changed so much over the past ten years or more, I'm not sure my grandparents could have adapted so easily with the world today. Although I've changed in my appearance and attitude, my love for the town in which I have grown up in has remained constant. Wherever I choose to live in the years to come, Morriston will always be home and Morriston is where I'd like to end my days (give or take seventy years!).

The passion flower (above) is a tribute to Morgan Tonen (1917–1987).

Acknowledgements

I would like to thank Miss Susan Beckley, County Archivist at West Glamorgan Archive Service, for permission to reproduce photographs which are held by West Glamorgan Archive Service, and for the support I have received during the past fifteen years. Also to Kim Collis, ncipal Archivist and Gwyn Davies, Archivist Assistant, who were so patient and helpful the years of research required to produce these books.

anks for the use of photographs must go to Elaine and Stan Hope; Marjorie Martin; lle; Jim Watkins; Pamela Price; Ivor Davies; the late Alec Hyman, and my friend, Morris, who is much missed.

ke to mention John C. Barrett, who is a very special and caring person – me on the straight and narrow and tolerates my awful sense of humour.

must go to my parents Joan and Denzil who for the past thirty years e with their support and love.

n in my first book from 1988 (although originally written 'Many thanks to everyone who assisted with this book. the dog who didn't.' The dog was Tinker and he is also

André D. Scoville 2002